T0288422

Weather Wise

CONTENTS

NATIONAL
GEOGRAPHIC   Hampton-Brown

School Publishing

Words with <u>oo</u>, <u>ou</u>, <u>ew</u>

Look at each picture. Read the words.

oo ew
ou

Example:

n<u>ew</u>s

gr<u>ou</u>p

c<u>oo</u>l milk

hot s<u>ou</u>p

sp<u>oo</u>n

High Frequency Words

| been |
| down |
| hard |
| now |
| number |
| push |

Key Words

Look at the pictures.
Read the sentences.

The Wind

1. The wind has **been** blowing **hard**.
2. The wind will **push** the kite up.
3. **Now** the wind stops and the kite goes **down**.
4. The kite may go up and down a **number** of times.

A kite needs wind to fly up and down.

Phonics Games

NGReach.com

3

Weather Tools

by Bo Grayson

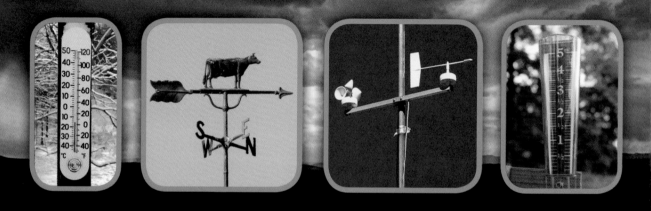

How can you tell what the weather will be? Here is a group of tools that can help.

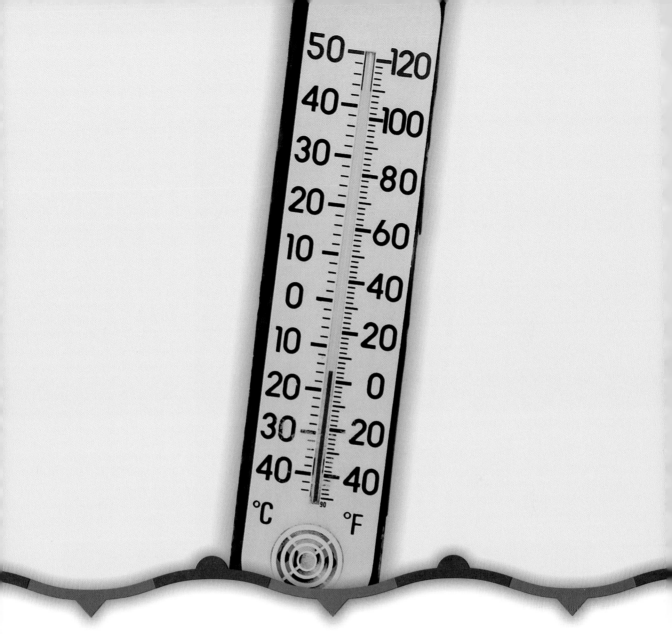

What can this tool do? It tells how hot
or cold the air is.

This tool has a smooth glass tube. The tube has liquid inside. The liquid goes up if the air gets hot. It goes down if the air gets cool. The numbers tell how hot or cold the air is.

What can this tool do? It shows which way the wind is blowing.

arrow

This tool sits on the roof of a house or barn. The wind pushes the arrow. Now the arrow is aimed where the wind is blowing. The wind may bring good or bad weather with it.

What can this tool do? It shows how fast the wind is blowing.

This tool sits on the roof, too.
It spins in the wind. It tells the wind
speed. If the wind blows hard, the
weather may change soon.

What can this tool do? It shows how much rain we get. This tool catches rain. The numbers show how much rain there has been.

SEVEN DAY FORECAST

SUN	MON	TUE	WED	THU	FRI	SAT
86	82	72	75	66	73	82
93	90	82	77	73	79	82

You might see this on the news.

It can tell you what the weather will be.

What day will you like best? ❖

Words with oo, ou, ew

Read these words.

tool	group	blew	hot
fast	cool	felt	news

Find the words with **oo**, **ou**, or **ew**. Use letters to build them.

t	o	o	l

Talk Together

Choose words from the box to tell your partner what each weather tool told.

This tool told that the air _felt_ _cool_.

1.

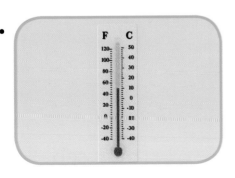

2.

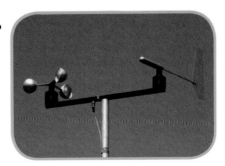

Words with <u>ue</u>, <u>ui</u>, <u>u_e</u>, <u>ew</u>

Look at each picture. Read the words.

Example:

s<u>ui</u>t

gl<u>ue</u>

t<u>u</u>b<u>e</u>

st<u>ew</u>

fr<u>ui</u>t j<u>ui</u>ce

bl<u>ue</u> cup

14

High Frequency
Words

| been |
| down |
| hard |
| now |
| number |
| push |

Key Words

Look at the picture.
Read the sentences.

The Boat Race

1. A **number** has **been** painted on each boat.
2. The wind swoops **down** **hard**.
3. It will **push** the boats.
4. **Now** the boats go fast to the end.

Which boat will win? What number does the boat have?

Phonics Games
NGReach.com

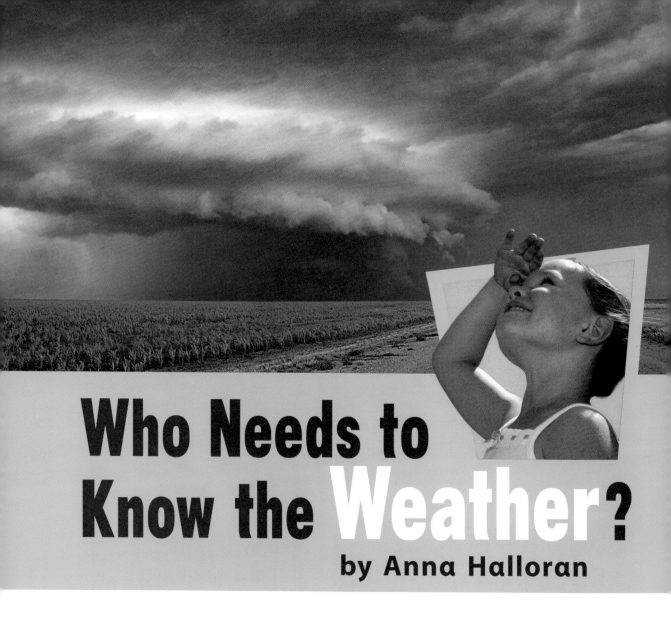

Who Needs to Know the Weather?

by Anna Halloran

What will it be like outside? Are blue skies due? Will it be hot or cold?

Who needs to know?

We all need to know.

farmer

wet fields

Farmers need to know the weather.
Is it time to plant crops now? If it rains
too much, crops cannot be planted. The
fields will be too wet.

land

If it has been dry, crops cannot be planted. The land will be too hard.

fruit

fruit

Will it get cold at night? Fruit on trees can freeze. Ice can bruise the fruit.

Sailors need to know the weather.
Is it safe to sail a boat? Strong winds can
make huge waves in the sea. Close to
land, the waves can push a boat onto
the sand.

tube

Out at sea, huge waves can smash a boat. These sailors need help. A rescue team drops a tube down. They lift the sailors off the boat.

raincoat

boots

You need to know the weather. Check for a few clues. Will it rain? Get a raincoat and boots.

snowsuit

mitten

Will it snow? Get a snowsuit and mittens. Will it be hot? Dress to stay cool.

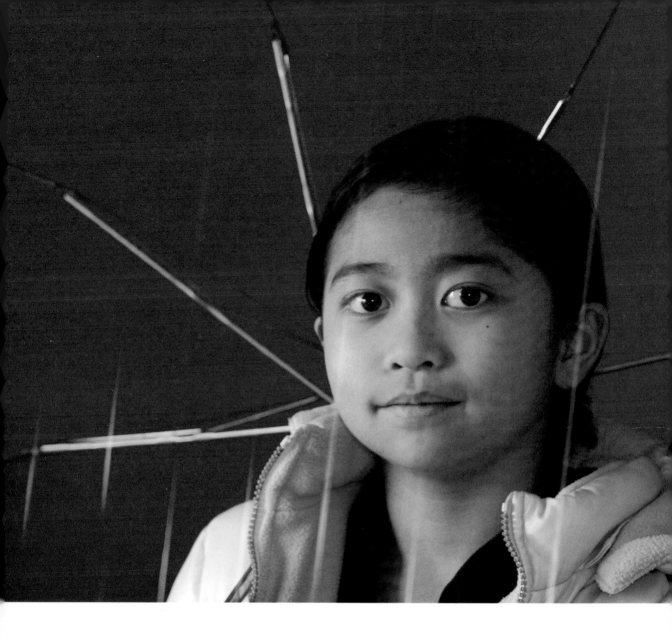

It's true! We all need to know
what the weather will be. What is your
weather like? ❖

Words with <u>ue</u>, <u>ui</u>, <u>u_e</u>, <u>ew</u>

Read these words.

few	blue	clues	fruit
pie	glue	seeds	tube

Find the words with
ue, **ui**, **u_e**, or **ew**.
Use letters to build them.

Talk Together

This ___fruit___ has a ___few___ seeds.

Choose words from the box
to complete the sentences.

1.

This _____ has
a _____ seeds.

2.

This _____ is
_____.

3.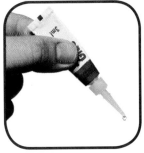

This _____ is
in a _____.

Which Weather Tool Is It?

Look at the weather tools with a partner. Read all the clues. Find the tool that matches all the clues.

1 You put this tool outside.

2 This tool does not tell how hard the wind blew.

3 It does not sit on the roof.

4 It has a group of numbers on it.

5 It has a smooth tube.

6 Rain does not go down the tube.

7 The numbers tell how hot or cool it is now.

Acknowledgments
Grateful acknowledgment is given to the authors, artists, photographers, museums, publishers, and agents for permission to reprint copyrighted material. Every effort has been made to secure the appropriate permission. If any omissions have been made or if corrections are required, please contact the Publisher.

Photographic Credits
CVR (Cover) Alaskastock/Photolibrary. **2** (b) William Berry/Shutterstock. (tl) Corbis/Jupiterimages. (tr) DNY59/iStockphoto. **3** (b) Liz Garza Williams/Hampton-Brown/National Geographic School Publishing. (t) Yi Lu/Corbis. **4** (bg) Digital Vision/Getty Images. (cl) Jason Cheever/Shutterstock. (cr) Tony Freeman/PhotoEdit. (l) David Hardman/iStockphoto. (r) Darryl Brooks/Shutterstock. **5** David Hardman/iStockphoto. **6** David Hardman/iStockphoto. **7** Jason Cheever/Shutterstock. **8** Jason Cheever/Shutterstock. **9** Tony Freeman/PhotoEdit. **10** Tony Freeman/PhotoEdit. **11** Darryl Brooks/Shutterstock. **12** jamaican/Shutterstock. **13** (bl) Martin McCarthy/iStockphoto. (br) Drazen Vukelic/iStockphoto. (t) Liz Garza Williams/Hampton-Brown/National Geographic School Publishing. **14** (bl) Susan Trigg/iStockphoto. (br) Shane White/iStockphoto. (cl) Benoit Beauregard/iStockphoto. (cr) PhotoDisc/Getty Images. (tl) Alexey Nikolaew/Shutterstock. (tr) C Squared Studios/Photodisc/Getty Images. **15** (b) Liz Garza Williams/Hampton-Brown/National Geographic School Publishing. **16** Digital Vision/Getty Images. (inset) Gloria-Leigh Logan/iStockphoto. **17** wrangel/iStockphoto. (inset) PhotoDisc/Getty Images. **18** Colleen Bradley/iStockphoto. **19** Value Stock Images/Unlisted Images. (inset) Wayne Eastep/Getty Images. **20** (b) Justina Sevostjanova/iStockphoto. (t) PhotoDisc/Getty Images. **21** Patrick Eden/Alamy Images. (inset) AndyL/iStockphoto. **22** (bg) Digital Vision/Getty Images. (fg) Stockbyte/Getty Images. **23** (l) Image Source/Corbis. (r) Polka Dot Images/Jupiterimages. **24** Edwin Verin/Shutterstock. **25** (bc) PhotoDisc/Getty Images. (bl) Artville. (br) Clayton Hansen/iStockphoto. (t) Liz Garza Williams/Hampton-Brown/National Geographic School Publishing. **26** (l) Paulo Cruz/iStockphoto. (r) EuToch/iStockphoto. **26-27** (bg) Clint Spencer/iStockphoto. **27** (br) ERproductions Ltd/Blend Images/Jupiterimages. (tl) Stephen Coburn/iStockphoto. (tr) Vivian Delmotte/iStockphoto.

Illustrator Credits
15 Nomar Perez

The National Geographic Society
John M. Fahey, Jr., President & Chief Executive Officer
Gilbert M. Grosvenor, Chairman of the Board

National Geographic School Publishing
Hampton-Brown
www.NGSP.com

Printed in the USA.
RR Donnelley, Menasha, WI

ISBN: 978-0-7362-8044-0

16 17 18 19
10 9 8 7 6 5 4

New High Frequency Words	Target Sound/Spellings	
been down hard now number push	**Vowel Digraphs** **oo, ou, ew**	**Vowel Digraphs** **ue, ui, u_e, ew**
	Selection: **Weather Tools** cool group news roof smooth soon too tool(s) you	**Selection:** **Who Needs to Know the Weather?** blue bruise clues due few fruit huge rescue snowsuit true tube